Angel Baby Girl - Copyright © 2024 by Julie Rendon.

All rights reserved. Published in the United States of America by Julie Rendon.

No part of this publication may be reproduced, distributed, or transmitted in any form or by any means, including photocopying, recording, or other electronic or mechanical methods, without the prior written permission of the copyright owner.

The US Library of Congress has established a Cataloging-in-Publication record for this title.

Library of Congress Control Number: 2025900476

ISBN: 979-8-218-58996-7 (Kindle eBook)

ISBN: 979-8-9925169-1-3 (Hardcover)

Printed in the United States of America - (1st Printing, 2024)

For information about permission to reproduce selections of this book,
write to Permissions, Julie Rendon via email: JulieRendon206@gmail.com

Demi

Dedicated to Demi, our beautiful angel baby girl. Thank you for the joy and laughter. I'm grateful for the years you were with us. We will always cherish you. With all our love, your parents,
Mario and Julie

Julie & Mario

Dedicated to my wonderful husband, Mario. Thank you for your kindness and love as I wrote this book about Demi. You conjured up memories of our furry daugher's goofy and happy personailty. Thank you for being an amazing daddy to our beautful girl.

Patrick & Spot

Dedicated to our dear friend, Patrick. His amazing artistic talent and expertise in the field of technology brought this book to life. I'm forever grateful for you and your friendship.

Chapter 1
A Prayer

*I grew up with dogs,
they were my wonderful friends.
Each one was special,
they were a Godsend.*

*We would play fetch and chase.
They were so fast they always won the race.*

*When my furry friends got sick, I cried.
I did not want to say goodbye.
Though I was sad, I had peace.
In heaven, their illness would cease.*

*At God's home, they were healthy,
happy, and could roam.*

All Rights Reserved © 2024 Julie Rendon

Pepper   Corky   Spanky

*Pepper, Corky, and Spanky too,
my furry blessings, I love you.*

*You left memories of joy and laughter,
they are in my heart forever after.*

*Now grown, without a doggie to love,
I prayed for a special puppy from God above.*

Chapter 2
Puppies!!

A man was selling puppies outside the grocery store.

When I saw them, I swung open the car door.

I ran to the adorable bundles of joy. The Border Collie puppies looked like plump, doggy toys.

*The moment I picked you up
I knew you were mine.*

*I would adore and love you
until the end of time.*

*I held you close
until your fur tickled my nose.*

*I let out a great, big ACHOO
I felt down to my toes.*

*Walking through the parking lot,
 you gave a little cry.*

*I did not want you to be scared,
 so I sang a lullaby.*

*Wrapped in my raincoat,
 warm, safe, and dry
quickly, you were asleep
 as cars rushed by.*

Chapter 3
Your Name

*There wasn't a name
as beautiful as you,
we decided Deming
would nicely do.*

*Daddy told me I said
your name in the night.
Pretty little girl,
you were our delight.*

*I whispered your name
with such love,
you could only be a gift
from God above.*

Chapter 4
Nap Time

*You fell asleep in daddy's shoe.
Some of your body was out of view.*

*Up was your little derriere.
We giggled at the sight
of your bottom in the air.*

*You woke and stared as if to say,
"When my nap is done, we will play."*

Chapter 5
Oh No!

It was a cool autumn morning.

You and I wanted to play,
but I had to go to work
so I could not stay.

To keep you warm,
safe, and dry,
I put you in your cozy bed
and then said goodbye.

The hands of the work clock seemed
stuck at a quarter past nine.
I wish I had the power to speed up time.

I imagined playing tug-of-war with you.
There is nothing more I'd rather do.

*Work was over; the day was done.
I wanted to be with you and have some fun.*

*Before I drove up the long, windy road,
I decided to surprise you with a doggy bone.*

*I went to the pet store,
and bought yummy treats
and squeaky toys galore.*

*I sped up the mountain road so eager to be with you.
I didn't see the stop sign; I accidentally went through.*

*When I got home, I opened the door with a burst.
You were asleep, I saw you first.*

You opened your big, brown eyes.
You looked at me with surprise.

Then you sprang from your warm, soft bed.
I wanted to hold you, but instead,

you ran in circles so fast
I smiled and laughed at last.

That is, until you slid to a stop
into my grandma's china box.

*The dishes went CRASH
on the concrete floor.
It was so loud it shook our door.*

*"Oh No, Deming! Grandma's
china was wrapped for 50 years!"
I was so sad I broke into tears.
I picked you up and held you near.*

*Our embrace replaced what made
me sad, and just like magic,
my heart was glad.*

Chapter 6
Yuck!

One day our handyman
was at our home.
Excited to meet you,
he brought you a bone.

You wiggled and jiggled
as he walked towards you.
With every step,
your excitement grew.

*Once upon you,
he stroked your little head.
That did not calm you, but instead
you squealed and stirred in my arms
until pee-pee flowed down to my alarm.

The front of my white shirt
was now stained yellow
which made the handyman laugh
because he was a happy fellow.*

Chapter 7
Playtime

*Daddy loved to play fetch with you.
He laughed at what you wouldn't do.*

*Daddy threw the ball with such might.
You wanted to catch it, so you immediately took flight.*

*Your black ears bounced in the air,
to catch that bright, yellow ball was your only care.*

*Once at the end of the patchy, green grass
you caught the ball with a quick grasp.*

*You dropped the ball between your paws as
if to say, "I've won the game, so that's all."
Daddy said, "Demi. The game is not done,
let's continue our fun.*

*You must bring the ball back to me,
so we can play fetch; it's fun, you will see."*

You tilted your head and wagged your tail
as if to say, "Daddy, I did not fail.
I won the game, I caught the ball
let's play our water game. Do not stall!"

Daddy positioned the old faded hose
above his head and not at his toes.

He squeezed the blue nozzle with such force
water shot out and followed a course
up to the massive pine tree
that stood tall behind you and Daddy.

*The SPLAT of water
on sharp pine needles
dropped them to the ground
along with some scary, dark beetles.*

*You were so excited to play,
and seemed to shout
"Pokey pine needles
and scary black beetles,
go far away
because it's Water Game Day!"*

*Daddy held the hose
gently above your nose.
Drinking water in midair
with your usual flair*

*made the water hit ground
with a splashing sound
landing on the pine needle mound.*

*Soaked by playing this game over and over
Daddy brought it to closure.*

*Under the warm sun
we were all having fun
you shook off water drops,
until there none.*

*With a gleam in your eye
you saw brown bunnies pass by.
They hopped with all their might
under our red deck and out of sight.*

You jumped on our deck
and hopped like a bunny.

We all giggled
you were so funny.

The bunnies wouldn't play.
They stayed under the deck all day.

Still you had fun because
you bounced on the deck
for the rest of the day.

Chapter 8
Welcome Buddy

*I saw a blond puppy
on the school playground.
He was so cute
as he wandered around.*

*Desperately,
I wanted to love this little guy.
My students were aware
I couldn't tell him goodbye.*

*Wanting to help me,
my students shouted on the phone
"Please let her
take this cutie home!"*

With shock and surprise,
"Daddy said, "Okay".
You now have a brother
with whom you will play.

Our tiny puppy named Buddy
was safe in the car.
I placed him in a shoebox
so he couldn't go far.

When we got home
you looked up with glee,
and with your eyes exclaimed,
"For me?"

Chapter 9
Dinner

*Deming,
you were our big girl then.
Your enormous hunger
never seemed to end.*

*You took a bite
out of everything in sight
from baskets, to carpet, to plants,
even Daddy's pants.*

*There was no end to how
much you could eat.
You seemed to think
everything was your treat.*

*You! Ripped the leather on
Grandpa's green recliner;
pulled out the white stuffing,
the damage was not minor;*

*You! Gnawed on Grandma's
antique cedar chest;
chomped on the brown side table,
oh what a mess;*

*You! Chewed the legs and seat
of the tan dining chair;
munched the kitchen cabinets,
oh what a nightmare.*

*We picked up the mess
until the family room was neat.
It was 6 o'clock and time to eat.*

*Mommy and Daddy
ate dinner at their table.
You and Buddy
were beside us and able.*

*Waiting for food
to fall from our plates,
neither of you waited with grace.*

*Drool dripped from your lips,
and landed on Buddy's head
without a miss.*

*Buddy's head was wet and icky.
His golden fur was so very sticky.*

*We wiped away the slobber
hoping there would be no more,
but soon a line of your
saliva fell to the floor.*

Chapter 10
Counter-Surfing

You smelled something yummy
and you wanted to fill your tummy.

So, you made the decision
to run into the kitchen.

You stood on your hind legs
and placed your front paws
on the tile with a smile.

Then, you hopped down
the counter to and fro
to reach the rising dough.

You slid the gray pan closer to you
and decided the golden dough
was ready to chew.

"CRASH!" went the metal pan
when it hit the floor.
It scared you so,
you ran out the door.

Daddy's dough
was on the ground.
That beautiful bread-to-be
was spread all around.

The dough
went into the trash.
Our hopes of eating the bread
were now dashed.

*No more counter-surfing for you!
So this is what you decided to do.*

*You sat next to Daddy hoping
he would give you a treat.
Oh, how you wanted to eat.*

*You licked
Daddy's fingers,
But the hot spice
did not linger.*

Daddy said,
"Deming. I am not a chew toy.
Please stop nibbling my arm,
oh boy!"

You did not quit
so Daddy made you sit.

He slathered his arm
with red spicy sauce
thinking you would stop
because it was hot.

The chili sauce
did not stop you.
You loved it!
There was nothing
else we could do.

Chapter 11
What Was That?

*It was a cold Friday night,
we had an enormous fright.*

*There was a CRASH
as loud as could be.
It was dark,
and we could not see.*

*We put you on a leash,
to lead us through our home,
but you shook like a mouse
and ran into your kennel house.*

We could not ignore the THUD
we heard the night before.
I, being the bravest,
slid open the thick glass door.

I stepped into the chilly backyard
and immediately spied
the old Mulberry tree
lying on its side.

It hit the metal roof
of the tool shed
before it came to rest
in our garden bed.

Chapter 12
Angel Baby Girl

*Daddy had surgery
to remove his wisdom teeth.
On the way home,
you did not leave him alone.*

*He was swollen
for days one, two, and three.
You stayed by his side
with your eyes opened wide.*

*You watched his every move,
you knew he was sick.
When Daddy felt pain,
you gave him a lick.*

You slept beside Daddy
for three days and nights.
By the fourth morning,
Daddy was alright.

This is how you became known
as our Angel Baby Girl.
You will always be our gem,
our diamond, and our pearl.

Chapter 13
Scary Animals

One day Uncle Kiko took you and your little brother Buddy, for a walk.

You didn't even make it halfway around the block.

When you heard the 'meow' of a cat close to the trees you darted behind your uncle's knees.

Uncle Kiko laughed
because you were the big girl
of our small pack.

Little Buddy barked
and growled at the cat
in the tall oak tree.

You seemed to say,
"Thank you, little brother,
for protecting me."

Later that night you heard
the 'who, who' of the owl
that lived in our tall pine tree.

You looked up in fright
and hoped it would flee.

You darted behind Daddy in fear
hoping the owl would not fly near.

As you whimpered and whined Daddy laughed because he knew all would be fine.

The magnificent owl with its great wingspan flew away as you ran.

Chapter 14
The Groomer

We took you to the groomer
against your will.
Your nails needed to be clipped,
but you were not thrilled.

You loved to roll
in the dirt and dust.
To the stinky smell,
we could not adjust.

The groomer tried
not to giggle
as you wiggled
to get away.

You wouldn't stay.

As you soaked in the bath
the groomer laughed.
You stayed alert
as she scrubbed the dirt.

*When we picked you up
you hopped into
the back seat of the car.
We were shocked
that you pooped
before we got very far!*

*Daddy was mad
but mommy said,
"Oh let her be.
She's our sweet
angel baby girl
and is precious to me."*

Chapter 15
Christmas

We decorated our pine Christmas tree, it was a beautiful sight for all to see.

A special adornment hung from a limb, a starfish ornament that once did swim.

*We raced home
to our beautiful gift of joy,
our starfish ornament
had become your toy.*

*It no longer dangled
from our Christmas tree,
bits and pieces were scattered
for all to see.*

*It was Christmas morning
and time to open your gifts.
It was funny watching
you take a few sniffs.*

*You spotted the present
you wanted to open first.
You ripped open the red package
and gave an outburst…*

*You pulled your
toy globe apart
piece by piece.*

*Our hopes for
its future ceased.*

*"Deming ate the world,"
Mommy and Daddy
would say.*

*We could not be happier
then to see you play.*

Chapter 16
The Phone Call

*Daddy called me
at work one day.
This was strange,
I must say.*

*He said, "Our beautiful
Angel Baby Girl is sick.
Please come home
and be quick.*

*The vet said Demi's
kidneys are failing."
When I heard that,
I began wailing.*

*I was sad and scared
of losing you,
I said many prayers
to get me through.*

*I slept with you each night.
My arms wrapped
around you tight.*

*The day came when
we said goodbye to you,
it was the hardest thing
we had to do.*

*Without any pain
you drifted off to sleep
while Daddy and I
continued to weep.*

Chapter 17
Heaven

*Eight years full
of joy, love, and laughter,
were our memories
of you to keep ever after.*

*For God had called you home,
now in Heaven,
you could painlessly roam.*

*God heard me pray
night after night.
He answered my prayers
by giving me insight.*

*I understood
I'd see you in my dreams…
hopping with bunnies,
oh, so funny.*

*Playing with cats
you once hid from,
dear friends,
you have become.*

*Unafraid of the owl
who lived in our
tree long ago,
echoing his 'who who'
that once scared you so.*

Chapter 18
You'll Always Be With Me

Angel Baby Girl
will always be with me.

When I …
hear little whimpers just like hers;
touch something soft as her fur;
see a ball like her globe
that is chewed apart instead of whole;
witness glass falling to the ground
like Grandma's china which gave a huge, loud sound.

All these things came to be,
that is how I know Angel Baby Girl will always be with me.

Julie Rendon is a retired schoolteacher who lives in Half Moon Bay California with her husband Mario, and her two furry children Lindy and Billy. Lindy and Billy provide hours of joy and laughter eight days a week.

Julie earned her Bachelors Degree and multiple teaching credentials from Notre Dame de Namur University and her Masters in Education from California State University Fresno. She also enjoys crocheting, embroidery, and baking.

www.ingramcontent.com/pod-product-compliance
Lightning Source LLC
Chambersburg PA
CBRC102342090526
44582CB00015B/192